A Sleep That Is Not Our Sleep

ANHINGA PRESS

A Sleep That Is Not Our Sleep

E.C. Belli

2020 Philip Levine Prize for Poetry
Selected by Cathy Park Hong

ANHINGA PRESS
TALLAHASSEE, FLORIDA 2022

Cover Image: "The Room," 2015 by Nanse Kawashima.
        www.nansekawashima.com

Type Styles: Text and titles set Adobe Jensen Pro Light,
        designed by Robert Slimbach

Library of Congress Cataloging-in-Publication Data

A Sleep That Is Not Our Sleep by E.C. Belli—First Edition

ISBN—978-1-934695-73-9

Library of Congress Cataloging Card Number—2021936330

Anhinga Press Inc. is a nonprofit corporation dedicated wholly to the publication and appreciation of fine poetry and other literary genres.

For personal orders, catalogs, and information, write to:

ANHINGA PRESS
P.O. Box 3665 ✦ Tallahassee, Florida 32315
Website: www.anhingapress.org ✦ Email: info@anhinga.org

Published in the United States by Anhinga Press
Tallahassee, Florida ✦ First Edition, 2022

to P.P., winged

THE PHILIP LEVINE PRIZE FOR POETRY

The annual competition for the Philip Levine Prize for Poetry is sponsored and administered by the M.F.A. Program in Creative Writing at California State University, Fresno.

2020
E.C. Belli
A Sleep That is Not Our Sleep
Selected by Cathy Park Hong

2019
Steven Kleinman
Life Cycle of a Bear
Selected by C. G. Hanzlicek

2018
Mark Irwin
Shimmer
Selected by C. G. Hanzlicek

2017
Tina Mozelle Braziel
Known by Salt
Selected by C. G. Hanzlicek

2016
Rachel Rinehart
The Church in the Plains
Selected by Peter Everwine

2015
Andrea Jurjević
Small Crimes
Selected by C. G. Hanzlicek

2014
Christine Poreba
Rough Knowledge
Selected by Peter Everwine

2013
Chelsea Wagenaar
Mercy Spurs the Bone
Selected by Philip Levine

2012
Barbara Brinson Curiel
Mexican Jenny and Other Poems
Selected by Cornelius Eady

2011
Ariana Nadia Nash
Instructions for Preparing Your Skin
Selected by Denise Duhamel

2010
Lory Bedikian
The Book of Lamenting
Selected by Brian Turner

2009
Sarah Wetzel
Bathsheba Transatlantic
Selected by Garrett Hongo

2008
Shane Seely
The Snowbound House
Selected by Dorianne Laux

2007
Neil Aitken
The Lost Country of Sight
Selected by C. G. Hanzlicek

2006
Lynn Aarti Chandhok
The View from Zero Bridge
Selected by Corrinne Clegg Hales

2005
Roxane Beth Johnson
Jubilee
Selected by Philip Levine

2002
Steven Gehrke
The Pyramids of Malpighi
Selected by Philip Levine

2001
Fleda Brown
Breathing In, Breathing Out
Selected by Philip Levine

CONTENTS

ACKNOWLEDGMENTS

Grateful acknowledgment is made to the journals and editors who first featured these poems (sometimes under different titles and in different iterations):

The Antioch Review: "Etymology"

Dark Sky Magazine: "Wick Effect"

DIAGRAM: "Wants" and "Persistence"

Fire Poetry Magazine (UK): "A Short History" and "Idyll in
        Slow Motion"

lafovea: "Illumination"

Deepest thanks to Mai Der Vang and Jefferson Beavers at California State University, Fresno, for their support, and also to the readers of the Philip Levine Prize. To Kristine Snodgrass and Carol Lynne Knight for their work on this: many thanks. And to Cathy Park Hong, for giving this volume the chance to be, I am deeply grateful.

Gratitude goes to the Paul & Daisy Soros Fellowship for New Americans for their enduring support. To Nanse Kawashima, who lent her beautiful art to this cover: my deepest appreciation. To Claire, James, and Andrew: to get to love you in this life is beyond any privilege I could have envisaged. To all the kind souls who have helped me grow in this craft, I am entirely indebted.

A Sleep That Is Not Our Sleep

UTOPIA

As the theory of the multiverse
Would have it
There is an infinity
Of worlds
Such as this one
In which every detail
Down to the whisker
Is identical
Except for one
In the world of always-summer
Which is just like this one
The trees are new, and the sky
Is moveable
Houses blend, years meld
Your friends love you, your parents
Call every Sunday with questions
Suggesting real interest
In your ever-changing passions
You are still you, very much so,
But the past is the past
And the children are full
Of forgiveness

He eats a sleep that is not our sleep.
— *Djuna Barnes*

I

CONSECRATION

Enter light & its mire
Daybreak in full gloom
Here we are, gradual foxes
in long forests of sorrow
And the moon—what an absurdity
Our fern-rimmed faces
livid with tenderness
I know how to die—
I've learned everything
through skin
(Don't all women?)
But then you found me asleep again
making a territory
of myself, quite lovely
for me alone

LAMENTATION

The certainty of rain: what a wonder.
Something to rely on,
the assurance of gloom
softly visiting
in the afternoon.
The most you'll give
is a vow
that the knives won't blossom
for now—
but the ones you have get to stay.
What about *days*?
I like mine tall, dark, and rainy
like Borodin.
The kind that devastates you
without saying a word.
Milk is a promise you made me.

CONSOLATION

This haste of razors
leaves me worn
but valiant with hair
Face of bark
All these rooms overlapping
in my memory
are soiled with hope
How about some moonlight
for a change—
It's softer
on the soul
But you're hot on the trail
of my wrongs again
(we—the beautiful, lovesick
blooms)
Do you remember,
how we were once a moving
tribute
to the ancient realms
of humanity & its burgundy
abandons

BLESSING

You abandoned me in a hurricane
(that part is littoral)
even after your dream (*I dreamed,*
you said,
that the children left the house
in the night
and marched
into the ocean)
Why are limbs so trivial
in your reality?
You were once my white
pebbles in the light
of the moon,
you'd help me back—
my erotic
forearms, an elegy
for frost
That was before
I found my joy,
clawed
& cowering in this truce
of elms where
none of it is love

ANTICIPATION

The afternoon, maternal lump
of colorless red
The occasional benevolent
glint, urged flare
of sunlight
The beach and its sullen hair
of blue
You've brought your worn indifference,
its wretched soliloquies
And here I am
with my pale intimacies—
somehow moved
by you
I've brought too a biting crowd
of desire
We are all foolish
and desperate,
over-eager and
prepared,
undressed, with a towel
over the arm
stepping into
another endless thread
of languid Sundays

ELEMENTS

The mist evangelizing before the sun
What a wreck of weather—
The forge from whence I grew
Here I am, rising
Out of morning
Into a continuous ruin
Another tranquil parting
Show me the roses
Take my hand

ETIQUETTE

Sorrow is more alluring
when it is
complete—
Could you please
hand it back
with the salt

ETYMOLOGY

For a long time I thought
there was something

wrong
with the definition of child—

the role assigned
seemed simple enough

but when I failed yet again
I began to think

there was something
wrong

with me. There are many things
I've forgotten:

the walk
through the statues

at breakfast, the walk
through the marble

at bedtime, that sense
of being created

a bird bath and you
are the rain that never comes.

II

BILLET DOUX

Hum a little, Mr. Bones.
    —*John Berryman*

Sometimes, you are a colander, losing things.
    — *Aracelis Girmay*

Dear Bones: had I known

of course

I would have

    let you out

Dear Bones:
the light
the light
the light

Dear Bones: you go!
I'll catch up—
          it's only a pair
of eyes
there
on my trodden face

two lumps of night

don't worry,
Bones:
I'll drag them out

Dear Bones: sorry

I couldn't let you go—

try to
understand

if you went, what of mine

would be left
            to break?

                        *

Dear Bones: I've

already
taken out

the birds

            imagine the
silence now: a brain

absent

of feathers

18

Dear Bones: we are all just bad

(w)omen

I'm glad this punishment
came—

or is it still
coming?

someone fetch the priest

but he's sleeping!

with whispers down his
neck
& his old whiskers
down someone's

neck

clean him up, will you

we need him

Dear Bones: nobody wants
to spread ashes with you

couldn't you try to be
a little more,

I don't know,
pliable

                    *

Dear Bones: the priest?

Dear Bones: see my sleeves
their ironed fauna

why yes, my wrists
always were
            this erotic

roll them up & the world
of animals
is pulled in

like a tide

the light on my shoulder
is a lacquer

                    *

Dear Bones:
where were we going?

Dear Bones: give it
a rest

or resist

commit to the path—
it only takes
five minutes

a day

after day after
day, which adds

up to about
five-hundred years

we don't have

Dear Bones:
just wait

time cures
all

ills. I'll
find ways

not

to kill it

Dear Bones: Isou said it
he said

the letters

they're destined
to something else

than words

Dear Bones: I'll tell it to you straight
you too

are due
for some divergences
in your path

what will it be then—
fossil or

combustion
(sounds a bit

like a Spanish
dance—

so
charming,

no?)

Dear Bones: you tell him,
this time
we've had it

as alluring as you are
with your toothsome
grin, I'm not going
to let you shit on me

start packing, Bones!
I'll throw the

foxes & starlight
into boxes

and we'll
go

Dear Bones: if this is an escape
shouldn't you just

run
& leave

the boxes

this one, anyway
the cat peed in

                              *

Dear Bones: your white waxen glow   like the
submissive kindness of oxen

is made

for more

Dear Bones: what do you know

of audiences?

do they bend?

Dear Bones:
I hear sometimes they do
—their heads mostly—

to protest the world
softly

through the quiet mist
of their gaze

*

Dear Bones:

let's give them something

Bones: run now or it will be
too late

no hope even
of

a musician at the end
Bones: leave the

two lumps of night

and leap

Dear Bones:

Bones?

do you hear me?

Bones?

[*to the audience*]: I think they're gone

I grew a bone once

a small piece

in the shape
of a *demi lune*

where someone else
had broken theirs

little clavicle bone, you grew

things grow well in me

see, Bones?

it can't all be bad.

after thirty-three anyway,
you've got to take some

responsibility, Bones.

Bones,
if I now start speaking softly

will you stay?

Dear Bones: my voice

has been a storm to you
and I won't share my

tea or two
carrots

even after

all of your hope
was

lost at sea
somewhere off

Kitty Hawk

Dear Bones: what do you know
of the first flight

that splendid machine
that looked just like

a mountain of beautifully set & wet
Bones?

does it make you dream?

Dear Bones: what if
I promise

not to switch

the hot water you choose
to the cold

I use
for matters
of thrift

expenditures are quite dangerous
don't you know

Bones, try not to judge me so

the audience, Bones, the audience
they're waiting

with the quiet mist of their gaze
and the terrible hope in their heart
they're waiting for love or forgiveness or forgetfulness
(the delight of oblivion) or a less
deliciously dark feeling to fondle their core
they're waiting maybe for one of these things
or all at once (when were audiences ever measured
in their wants?)
Bones, they're waiting
but words won't do much, Bones
it's a lot of black and blue (reminds you of the heart, no, Bones?)

on a lot of white—and that's your hue, Bones

Dear Bones: you began
as 270

and by the time I laughed less
some of you

had fused
and now

it's you, Bones. 206, that's all of you
in all of your gorgeous
blaring
cream
quietude

Bones, you like cream?

it's the color I picked

Bones, of black and blue
I finally chose
black too—

ask me why, Bones

Dear Bones: it's because
it reminds me
of the two lumps of night
I left
without a light on
in their outside house
I left them
without a
fight
because nothing is mine
but you, Bones

time to head home

I've had it
& you

are making me pine
for foxes and boxes and starglow

Bones, let's hear the city
swallow
the black & blue

ask the audience to take
a piece of you
along

because Bones: we're gone.

RELATIVE LUMINOSITIES

I have made my peace
with going dark—
stepping down
the stoop
into the big soup
of night
faced with the insolent
intrinsic brightness
of stars
which is the final lesson
I will learn nothing from
knowing myself
incapable
of radiance—
I'm less natural,
more of a household
chemical:
flammable
& if misused
will stain
the skin

IN THE ABSENCE OF TENDERNESS

People started living in my house
They sometimes had bodies
Sometimes they were just their jolly old shadow selves
Rarely, they spoke
I had the hope of God for a short while
Now it's too much, I tell the lady who sits across from me
When the baby points at the window
And it's black outside
And he says *peur*
I wonder if he too will meet
The shadows themselves or their little grand-shadows
The ones the older shadows bounce on their lap
In the light of the Christmas tree
With so much hope
That they might grow
Into being
Properly terrifying
As is the custom

I AM WASHING THE DISHES

The water as hot as it will go
I enjoy this memory
Of fire—
You step in
Placing your hands above the dish I am
Cleaning (not
Breaking)
Taking more of what's ours to share
You switch to cold—
Fire
Is a waste

STONES

I am writing a memo
Things to remember
For Tuesday
How everything grounds me
How I am looking for lighter things
Information is good, in way of distraction:
Meadowgrass can reach down
Twenty feet
And some animals were found with stones
Inside their rib cage
To crush whatever
Bitter pills they swallowed
Although some ingest the stones for ballast
To better keep themselves
From returning to the surface—
These animals
I know

IN SITU

I got moving today
It came in recommended
From a friend who knows things
He hosts people two nights a week
Exercises with others
Is even lyrical
Under a night sky
He's complex, has many layers—
I sit at the piano and think
Of how some animals are mobile before they grow
And how, as adults, they won't move anymore
Same view of the ocean floor
Same currents batting them
Over and over
For their short eternity
Their lives all up
To a faraway wind

EVOLUTION

Fog can be *an atmospheric condition* or
a type of bewilderment—
I am asked to think of ways
In which I can keep it
From settling

I sing, I say, *I sing*—

It's affirming because I fill the room
In a way that is
Enjoyable to others
I offer something without taking
I sing softly (and only when the space around me

Feels lacking)

But don't you realize
You have inherent value
By *being,*
She says
Not merely through purpose—

What ramblings, I think

How can *being*
Have value in and of itself?

Unless you are
Something heart-wrenchingly beautiful
A deep-sea creature maybe
A coelacanth
A living history

Proof

Of our growing legs
Which we can use today
To outrun the fog

DELIBERATIONS ON JOY

It's like a low-grade fever
But perpetual
She explains
With the occasional flare-up
Low-grade melancholy
Everything tinted
Since the beginning
With a special sheen
Of blue
The concrete under my feet
That much colder
The question Mother asked
Accusing
The dog's eyes
Sadder
Because of something
I didn't do
Or did

*

If it's chronic, I ask
What's the path to hope—
I can't pretend I am the earth
Where early on
The sky was orange
I want to be grateful for everything
To use my blue
To make purple
To radiate joy
Well maybe that's just not you

SIGNIFIERS

There are no words left —
The last one you sent down
With a rope around its neck
It's held at depth by stones
In the black and gray mire
It's fine—
I say the wrong things anyway
And I'm so broken
I know only
How to break more, you say
Better to be void
Of weapons then
I'll hand them over
Willingly, the words
Even the ones I love
Like *Remembrance*
I'll give you too
My senseless name
I never liked it anyway
And the new ways I'll speak
Yes, the new ways
Are these thin
Beautiful streaks
Like train rails crossing
The pallid skin
And rabid
With relief
I imagine
Somewhere

Somehow
Perhaps even
At a station
Ordering a coffee
Or signing up
For rewards
Some people
Not me
Are standing
Enunciating
Proudly saying
Their name

HUES

Some undeniable facts about our world:
Diversity of life, reproduction, patterns
But also mimicry—
One thing posing
As another
To protect themselves,
Some animals
Wear their opponents' clothes
Little imposters without syndromes
Meanwhile we self-flagellate
On our happy days for being too like the sun
On our sad ones for being too like the shadows
Denying ourselves the right
To being shadow or sun because the role is already filled, somewhere
But I can assure you I have seen many
Shades of gray
And your hue
Is inimitable; it dances against the brick
Of the buildings
In a distinct manner that summons a haunting
And in the nighttime
It hosts
The most beautiful
Tints of blue
I read about these in a book once
On a wood floor
Sitting next
To you

VOWS

I've been cradling the heavy cat in the half-dark
For an hour
She likes how I make her feel
And I like her—
I was mean to the dog
And now he's dead
Well, not mean
Cold in moments
He could have used the warmth
I could tell and still did nothing about it
But in my life I must always pay
In good time
And so here I am
Paying
Which I am accustomed to
And anyhow I am happy
To pay for such horrors, such ill manners
Of my character
Even if I do blame you for it—
How can I empathize with anything
When you are the only mountain
For miles around
I've had to learn to be kind again
To uncoil my tendrils into the light
Sometimes I pretend you are not a person
But a stone (how could I love
People again, if I didn't?)
And I warn them: Children,
Don't learn from stones

They are too still
They are too sharp
Sometimes in the moonlight
They whisper terrible things

I V

SELF-PORTRAIT AS PASTORAL

You called me all flanks and napes
You called me off
To the cashmere moon
This winter is unusually cold I am told
Every winter in the wake
Of embittered zambonis
Who doubtless run the weather
Out of town with their little mechanisms
And fangs and bayonets
I was waiting for a word like hemispheres
To break my skin
What are you these days
Still contorted in the afterglow
Still missing the parade

MANY WORLDS THEORY

This is the unsolvable chaos
Of fog or kingdoms

The loved one sealed
In an opposite lifetime

Skin laid out each morning
As though the soul were preparing to flee

Then grizzly snow on the line
Herded, dull incantations

I remember you Heart
Do you

Remember me—
And the eyes barely mended into dials

WANTS

Another love story folded inside a pillbox
Another day of amorphous need

How each side fought itself in the dark by accident
And I am better now: moving

My arms in an aim to be
As persistent as the clothespins

Spinning like aerialists on the line
(I notice more the spoiled pallor of things)

And here your gloves are curled like real hands
On the highest shelf of the closet

Unattainable and sodden
They've retained no scent at all

Off the television a near-sacred woman
Bleating little sermons in verse

A SHORT HISTORY

I met you a colossus
Every beat of the moon caught on your naked back
From the start you hated carnations
I love that they remind me of my bloodstream
There were mornings of amberina, putrid gold
There was a time when my unprotected body came
    to greet you at the door
Why the monsters with long faces around our bed you ask
I love someone else now
A touching joy comes after the battering
I paw at the sun through the glass

LOYALTY

Last night I dreamed you were home
Reading a book on imaginary beings
While the web of human hair still clung
To the shower door

I am visiting the pool these days
Where my remarkable smell lingers
Despite the moisture
And I felt a man's heat in the water

Is it you again
Inviting me to touch others to feel you

The sad giants continue to walk me
Home, at dawn
You know they follow me

Everywhere as I move through
This grief with luminous constancy

IDYLL IN SLOW MOTION

I take the machete to the carriage
We build a cabin we make love in
In real life the great saws are singing
And it's cold on the water
An ancient nakedness is being held
Somewhere against its will—
What it must be
To swallow acres of sawdust
And spit tobacco juice into a glass
For now I unhook the sun, put it away
These capsules I take cause polyphony
You know: the apples rotting in their sunbath
Rot marvelously well

ILLUMINATION

Slowly I am learning
To settle instead

Of plummeting, to lift
Like the selfish

Dust when the door opens
And drift only

So far. I know
At last to rise and resign

Myself to what careful
Design borders me:

To live is to learn to be
Barely there,

To raise the wet
Psyche out of weed

And memory
In complete silence

To reach the hedge and realize
This great upheaval

Must never end
And one day just like that

To begin considering
The dahlias

NOTES

"In the Absence of Tenderness" is written after Franz Wright

"Hues" is dedicated to Beth

The third line of "Wants" references *The History of the Peloponnesian War* by Thucydides

ABOUT THE AUTHOR

E.C. Belli is the author of *Objects of Hunger* (SIU Press, 2019), winner of the 2019 Crab Orchard Poetry Series First Book Award. She is the translator of *I, Little Asylum* by Emmanuelle Guattari (Semiotext(e), 2014) and *The Nothing Bird: Selected Poems by Pierre Peuchmaurd* (Oberlin College Press, 2013). The recipient of a 2010 Paul & Daisy Soros Fellowship for New Americans, her work in French has appeared in *Europe: revue littéraire mensuelle* and *PO&SIE* (France), among others. She is also the author of the chapbook *plein jeu*.